AMERICA BEYOND THE WELL
poems and transformations

John Curl

AMERICA BEYOND THE WELL

poems and transformations

ISBN: 978-1-7335775-0-2

Homeward Press
Berkeley, CA
https://johncurl.net/

AMERICA BEYOND THE WELL

America Beyond the Well
American Eagle
Journeying to America
American Doodle
The American Dream
An American Tragedy
That's What Made America Great
America the Beautiful
America's Finest Hour
America Land of the Free
America's Promise
American Know How
Democracy in America
Discovering America
Only in America
The American Experience
The American Way
On A Day Like Tonight in America
American Roulette
American Make-Believe
Un-American
American Transitions
American Turnovers

Without contraries is no progression.
— William Blake

AMERICA BEYOND THE WELL

poems and transformations

AMERICA BEYOND THE WELL

America beyond the well,
along the dusty road,
the acrid, rust-red soil supporting
only an occasional small vineyard,
they strolled house to house,
arresting families.
We heard a great noise and
were all enveloped in a wall
of heat and steam, while
concrete balconies crashed
into parked cars, an officer
lowered a plastic bag over her
head while another ground a lit
cigarette into her arm.

The melting snow, semi-translucent
and shining in the lantern glow,
seemed to be carved out
of a block of amber.
We worked
our way back, following
a little creek, sucking on
twigs of sassafras
and radiant sunshine
until, fringed by majestic pines,
we reached the canyon edge
and lit the sacred fire.

Although the time scale was so
vast and the abuse of evidence
so complete as to render it
unlikely, the flutes
and rattles summoned a
universal healing.

It was a moment of return,
the ancient languages,
long declared extinct by the experts,
springing suddenly back to life.
All we had were elders, drums, spirits,
and what they told us.

AMERICAN EAGLE

American eagle soars above
the crater of the old volcano,
abandoned prayers
nebulous hypocrisy clouds
morning dew apologies
scattered one by one
over the vast expanse
of privatized air and water.
Sailors in clown makeup,
apparently on
orders from the city manager,
ransacking the branch
library and an adjoining
nursery school, crashing
outboard skiffs into
the collapsing docks and
flaming taxis into
the stores, car alarms blaring
for hours set off
by the blasts. Investigators are
still trying to reconstruct
the chain of events.
The remarkable irony,
especially in view
of their bizarre reproductive
habits, is that
the general public appears

no longer even curious about it.
At the bottom of a
sunken road with high sandy
banks lined with cattails,
egrets still balance on one foot,
rusted weather cocks still spin,
minor prophets still ride swans,
erotic raccoons still wash wild ginseng,
while beneath the surface
millions of worms still chew
the earth in search of healing,
tranquility, harmony.
American eagle soars above
the crater of the old
volcano, gazing into
the caldera and dreams
of restoring the waters.

JOURNEYING TO AMERICA

In what were once
some of the city's balmiest
middle-class neighborhoods,
the withered lawns and
abandoned homes groan,
beaten and betrayed.
Recovering credible evidence in
the chaos can be difficult,
journeying to America.
But following the lockdowns,
evacuations and manhunts,
dark hearted officials
rushed to the scene where
they stopped a random
vehicle in front
of hundreds of bystanders
forced the passengers,
to their knees.
journeying to America.
We walked through
clumps of stonewort,
hogwort, submerged
pondweeds, lapping ripples,
a cloud of swirling flies, when
a sudden gust whipped
the still waters into
eddies and currents,

sweeping wave upon wave of
breakers hurling
coincidental debris
from the disasters
against the innocent shore.
We sought only to
preserve the knowledge
of our culture,
respect for our mothers
and grandmothers.
Deep in the crypt
of the abandoned sewer line
we drank from
a pure spring inside
an undiscovered grotto,
journeying to America.

AMERICAN DOODLE

Back in simpler days
a *doodle* was a country bumpkin
and *macaroni* were
fancy Italian hat ribbons.

Now, over two centuries later,
nobody calls a feather *pasta*
any more, but
Mr Doodle is still riding into town,
still thinking himself quite the dandy,
only now he's mounted
on an armored missile.

Mr Doodle, keep it up,
American Doodle Dandy,
be nimble, Mr Doodle,
oh, that sublime noodling,
oh, rub your sweaty subprimes
all over those abandoned girls
hiding razors in their doe-eyed smiles,
mind that music
bust those moves
grind that step
down on your jackboots
up on your leg irons
don't mind the funereal rhythms
of those tasty dirges and laments

grieving in the GI cemeteries
behind the dance halls,
flaunt your bursting bombs,
toss your turkey plumes,
get randy
with all the widows weeping
around the collapsed walls
of smitheened hospitals
incinerated kitchens
amputated workers
shrapneled orphans
collateraled ghosts
screaming in torn party dresses
as thick as hasty pudding,
just keep it up, Mr Doodle
stick that tail feather
into the bloody bullet hole
in what's left of your dented helmet
and call it lasagna, linguini,
vermicelli, fettuccini, tortellini
or whatever the fuck
you want to call it,
and everything will
be just
American Doodle Dandy.

Yes, I'm an American Doodle Dandy,
American Doodle do and die, die and do.
Come munch with me

on my poison bullet candy,
in your every favorite flavor,
red, white, and blue.
I once had an American Doodle sweetheart,
she was my American Doodle Helen of Troy.
But then one day I drove to town
and shot the Constitution
and now
we're all that American Doodle boy.

THE AMERICAN DREAM

On an island in the green river
of the northwest valley,
on a humble plant, flowering in
early spring, a larva
molts its skin, transforming
into a nymph.
While bodies, some
still handcuffed, gagged,
and body parts pile up
at the morgue, colorful
bouquets of entry
and exit wounds,
lacerations, contusions,
acid burns, punctures.
The filing of serious charges
in such cases
have been rare
in the American dream.
Northern lights fire the horizon.
Lost dogs and stray families
search for food
following prophesies
prowl the night streets
of the American dream.

AN AMERICAN TRAGEDY

Two earth spirits
of the pristine forest
were killed
by trailside bombs during sunset.
The presumed bombers
apparently fled the scene
on dirt bikes
for an adjoining canyon
cracked up to be
a virtual no-man's land.

In other news,
death squads detained an
additional thirty-one math students,
security guards shot
fourteen laborers as they slept
in their pup tents,
celebrity bodyguards
dined on five civilians,
and an assistant professor
of south Asian music
harpooned two dolphins,
six yellow dogs, a mule,
an unarmed opossum,
sixteen house cats of various colors
and assorted birds.
After several commercials,

the pundits yelled at each other
hotly debating whether it was
a situation comedy or
an American tragedy.

THAT'S WHAT MADE AMERICA GREAT

The first day of autumn,
the gleam of sunset on the edges
of impenetrable clouds.
The d.a. hands over the deleted files
to the jackal handling
the investigation into himself,
the caliber, distance from which
the bullets were fired, and
angle of entry
proving it was the work of just
one deranged individual
who, reports confirm,
has committed suicide:
that's what made America great.
They zip the bodies into bags
and stack them neatly behind
the elegantly pruned hedges.
Ignited apparently as a distraction,
a brush fire lit by the bailiffs
on orders from the judge
burns hundreds of humble homes
and thousands of banned books
to the ground.
To assure that the rules of
global finance are favorable
to certain corporate interests,
after the barrage of seven mortar rounds,

masked men in police uniforms
grab people at random,
and herd them into waiting vans.
Suddenly, without warning,
thousands of children
in seemingly haphazard locations
defy all authority:
that's what made America great.
Sheer cliffs, stony beaches,
sandy dunes, tidal pools,
waves on a moonlit lake.
The stream bed a parched channel
of rocks and pebbles in March
without warning becomes
an unstoppable torrent in April,
spreading inexorably across
the full extent of the flood plain
into the forest.
The suddenly-moist forest floor
strewn with withered
debris of decaying trees
springs abruptly back to life.
Seed pods soak up just enough
concentrated energy, patiently wait
for the waters to subside,
for their inevitable moment in the sun.
A generation yearning for oases of normalcy
in the throes of everyday violence,
comes precipitately into maturity,

and realizes that the howling ghosts of
past defeats by the plutocracy
mean nothing
less than the call of the future
for heroes organizing resistance,
revolt, and revolution:
that's what made America great.

AMERICA THE BEAUTIFUL

Automatic weapons in the hands
of children roaming
the abandoned schools,
mortar shells striking
groups of tarred and feathered
construction workers seeking jobs;
pillage and rape on Main Street
by orders of
the senior commanders.
How events unfolded and
who might have been involved,
conspiracy theories flying wildly about,
the entire armed services
and chambers of commerce
issuing quick robust denials,
while shivering investigators
secretly pray
the bodies are never exhumed,
America the beautiful.
To bolster the crumbling dollar
the People's Representatives
bloat the military budget
and drain social programs.
Tight-lipped judges scramble
to defuse the explosive situation,
important forensic evidence
spirited away in

heavily armed humvees,
while in broad daylight in
an open field a hundred yards away
two gunmen shoot women.
Yet the children still plot
with cedar waxwings,
desert tortoises,
coastal scrub sage in the lower
reaches of the coast-hugging peaks,
yellow pine and mixed
evergreens coping with
the drought conditions,
chaparral seemingly impenetrable
yet home to worlds
of animals and insects,
a wintering ground for
diving ducks,
the phases of the moon,
Mars rising at sunset.
Is this our reward or our punishment,
America the beautiful?

AMERICA'S FINEST HOUR

The whirl of bats and moths
in the wizard's cave,
profound ignorance clings like a shadow
desperate salamanders glower
America's finest hour.
Officials deny the president's crimes,
martial law in Seattle
judges break out in running sores,
all night she dreams of scorpions
dour CEOs prattle
bouquets of cancer devour
America's finest hour.
A school of translucent tropical fish
dart in a different direction,
grebes build floating nests
from marsh vegetation,
the CIA denies all allegations.
The extent of the abuses
overcasts the sky with signs,
Eddie squeezes a rock
Marcia chants on the picket line,
water shut off in Baltimore
Pittsburg off limits
the guilty plead and cower,
prisoners watch meteorite showers,
America's finest hour.
Goons disarmed by moms,

Truth Commission trials press on,
harbor seals lounge on the dock
stratocumulus clouds display purple,
an ant explores a petal
following round the charmed circle,
a few intertwined twigs
in the bright center of the milky way,
lovers nestled in a secret bower
America's finest hour.

AMERICA LAND OF THE FREE

Caressed by eagle feathers
and bison hooves,
in free fall love with
dismantled spirits,
equal blessings perfecting
nectar for the ants,
unconditional rejoicing,
rebellious wild hibiscus,
the west wind whistling through
cornflowers and yellow squash,
freely dismantling and
equally reassembling
piles of autumn leaves
over abandoned graves in
America, Land of the Equal
Land of the Free.

It took a woman's sense of irony
to reopen the tense confrontation,
sheering off passionate facades
of buildings, toppling overpasses, reeking
panic in crowded basements and alleys.
Swarms of officials unhinged
for want of an exit strategy,
secretly scurrying in frantic circles
to save their own skins,
while publicly trying to

establish beyond any reasonable
doubt that the leaders of
the free world
under constitutional law,
were not behind these desperate plots.

It almost seems like a cosmic joke.
Our enemies hate America because
we are so free and equal
equal and free,
because we've got freedoms
they don't have,
because we are the exceptions
in an unjust world,
we are the American exceptionals.

Right, the exceptional cost of necessities
causes mothers to eat their
free and equal hearts out,
because we equally can't afford
to get sick or grow old.
Skittish guards in gas masks
freely menace school halls piled
equally high with garbage.
Pervasive mistrust and
seething anger rage
freely and equally through
the cities, the suburbs
and the countryside.

Traumatized recruits with assault rifles
freely avoiding the intersections,
equally wary of booby traps and
freely transmitted diseases,
while alongside the freeway
chickens peck freely
at the devastated lives
composting equally
in the dust and mud.

Thus as a last resort
to save freedom and equality
our leaders freely and equally declared
equality and freedom
suspended indefinitely,
a temporary state of
endless national emergency
in exceptional America,
Land of the Equal
Land of the Free.

AMERICA'S PROMISE

I pledge allegiance to
America's promise.
I pledge defiance to
America's lie.

Defiance to
duplicity on every TV channel,
advertising campaign atrocities,
purity eaten by betrayal,
lifetimes of wilting cancer bouquets,
gallows in every school yard,
shackles on every birth certificate,
blatant fraud in every political ad,
impunity always granted,
the CEO's indictment always postponed
always the coronation of prejudice,
always the dictatorship of bread,
always the deadly fear of truth.

I pledge defiance to
America's broken promises.
I pledge allegiance to
the promises of
windswept beaches,
the openness of wildflowers,
the joy of turbulent streams
elated with their own pure power,

the passion of gentle brooks
babbling about secret loves
and heartaches,
the purity of swallows
swooping among wisps of clouds,
the perfection of snowflakes
in a child's hand,
the energy of whirligig beetles
darting among water lilies
with tubular roots buried
deep below in the rich
muck of the pond bottom.
I pledge allegiance to
the thrill of lovers' ankles intertwined,
to once-estranged sisters rejoicing
in cottonwood trees,
to rare necklaces of many-colored stones
hanging on many-colored
necks of rare beauty,
to the justice of homeless prophets dancing
through abandoned warehouses,
to the healing jangle of jingle dresses
swaying at cosmic pow wows,
to the joy of social equity
among the excluded and downtrodden,
I pledge allegiance to
elders burning stock certificates,
to children overthrowing the oligarchy,
to the yet-to-be-fulfilled

American experiment,
to the revolutionary moment,
I pledge allegiance to
America's promise.

AMERICAN KNOW HOW

American know how
to rupture ancient walls with artillery shells,
mix drinking water with sewage,
descend into bloodletting
so quickly and totally that
even city workers on routine duties
are afraid to enter their own neighborhoods.
The marchers in black armbands,
the logging firms guided by deadly angels,
the owls sitting motionless almost invisible
waiting for an unsuspecting passerby,
the godfathers slitting wrists,
the wardens betraying the forests every minute.
Oily smoke spirals over
and over and over
the houses of all the children who have never
seen the sun.
Debates on the subject
at the sidewalk tables
outside the juicebar
have deteriorated into spitting contests,
while inside
our ancient family line
has exploded like a rotting watermelon.
American once knew how
to soothe a scorching tangle of emotions,
hands trembling, chest heaving,

knew how
to farm a little spread along
an oxbow cut off from
the river's course, the apparent
color a reflection of
sky or shoreline birches,
knew how
to raise generations of healthy children,
to praise spices, turtles, crystals,
to nurture fantasies of flowers
mother's milk carousels
fuschia astronomy
confessions of unending love,
the generosity of robins.
Waiting for grandfather, grandmother,
waiting for the return of
buffalo sustainers of life.
Somewhere deep inside
you can almost hear the rising murmur
of forgiveness grounded in melodies
of forgotten corners of
the inner heart of community.
American still know how,
American know how.

DEMOCRACY IN AMERICA

Ironically the gang
at the top are really just a few
punks. The time of the
oligarchs always starts like this,
unfolding in unthinkable ways
before our very eyes, with
everybody watching,
the news trickling out in spasms
reaching a crescendo when,
for example,
another five mortar rounds
kills nine, wounds forty
and mutilates the childhood of an entire
generation. Even as we speak they're
trying to destroy the evidence.
There is a continuing investigation,
of course. There always is.
Has there ever been democracy in
America? The once and future
democracy.
Perhaps it can be best understood
in the context of
of billions of years of geologic
development, during most
of which living organisms
closely resembled non-living matter.
This of course

does not necessarily
explain consciousness, intelligence,
ethics, or behavior.
No one can predict the exact moment
of the quake, but any reading of
history will tell you that,
strolling along the fault
pronghorn antelopes can hear
the schist and granite
grinding beneath. The quietest
breeze can suddenly whip into
a maelstrom, and the swiftest
stream can suddenly swirl into
a quiet pool of
democracy in America.

DISCOVERING AMERICA

Why is the English
language still an alien tongue
in this continent,
not understood by
American wind, water,
trees or birds?

Where is our collective
sense of outrage?
Why has there been
no discovery?
Are we afraid to
discover America?

Strawbosses hiding missiles in
polluted crawlspaces, pesticide skies
obscuring the depths of mystery,
elected officials, with elevated levels
of heavy metals and PCBs,
repressing the laughter of children.
Charred twisted parts of cars
and busses lie scattered nearby,
the passengers initially not knowing
whether they had been hit by
bombs or unspeakable truths.
Poison festers in the wounds.
It is only because

the historical crimes are so great,
that they're afraid to proceed
with America's discovery.

Over at the abandoned capitol,
standing in the ruins,
on any balmy evening,
you can almost see
the purified spirits of ordinary people
hurling truths at
business-suited gangsters,
you can almost hear
the false dreams
and self-destructing violins
of deceit still sobbing
somewhere in the distance.
(This scenario replays
over and over in my head).

Yet despite all this,
discovery is still possible.
Wild plants are still
edible after all these painful years.
Little twigs of
mullein stripped of bark
still have healing properties.
Ant cities still thrive
in the cracks in concrete.
The children still cry for joy

at secrets revealed.
All things are still possible.

The only way forward to
America's discovery is
to listen to the land.

ONLY IN AMERICA

Forces were extorting on a maximum scale
hide indoors or get out of town
shattered glass and crumpled concrete
scattered along the sidewalk
during the interrogation
light penetration is restricted
in the day's deadliest attack
bayoneting three
workers in an ice cream shop
they only called on the soldiers to
allow food and
medicine to enter the town and
compensate the farmers for
destroying their crops while
three quarters of biodiversity
was lost
probably forever,
only in America.
Hooded youths carrying cat tails
stalked defiantly past the burning cars,
rusted missiles and corroded bombs
in the warm night rain,
met at the secret elm
and continued on,
wiring bridges and mountain tunnels
with red peonies
confessing love to carousels

sleeping in green squash and mother's milk
engulfing buildings in swans
burning sweetgrass purification
praising beaver dams and lavender bouquets
elating finger lakes
into a state of generosity
embracing the devotion of young lovers
forgiving dispirited pear trees
leading the refugees
onto the dance floor
caressing the elderly into
smooth thigh harmony
kissing imperfect souls and bodies
beyond apologies,
only in America.

THE AMERICAN EXPERIENCE

We cannot afford to wait
until they cut down
the last acacia tree,
until the authorities finish
torching the last corner fish market,
looting the last family bakery,
until the last midwife is
sprawling dead in a corner
of the last library.
Each day the prisons keep on
overflowing with a generation
of young men and women,
mostly of color,
marginalized, disenfranchised,
victims of institutional entrapment,
thinking rightly or wrongly,
 that their only desperate
hope to escape
lies in crime or rebellion.
But this is nothing new.
All has been going on all along,
occasionally being reported,
and when it was reported,
reports were meant to be
systematically ignored
in the American experience.

While our full growth
and innate possibilities
are constantly hindered
by a lack
of clean food and water,
our patrons and supervisors
turn our mutilated bodies
into decoys by the side of the road,
cautionary tales to intimidate
any following our footsteps.
When all else fails,
they pretend to
honor the fallen warriors
by awarding medals to our next of kin.
This was not the first time that
the universe became unreachable in
the American experience.
Meanwhile the winds of the four directions
continue to frame the pageant
of your great grandmother's life.
Porcupine tends the fire
of the inexorable laws of
cause and effect.
An old metal water pail ignites
your sense of wonder.
Ceremonial messengers offer
a ghost feast in the rolling hills,
while timberlines sway in the wind,
and valleys lush with blackberries

and hawks taking flight
offer us the power
of the rainbow.

We cannot live in the absence
of legends germinating
the seeds of rebellion and renewal.
Our aching spirits and bodies
rejuvenate as we dream
of hardscrabble fields
suddenly bearing lush crops,
of turning injustice on its head,
of light autumn rains beginning to seep
into the dense walnut groves
of the American experience.

THE AMERICAN WAY

How could something like this happen?
I don't want to judge anyone, but
only what I read in the newspapers:
the vast majority shot
execution-style, others
beaten to death, strangled, bodies
pocked with drill-holes, burns,
missing eyes, teeth, nails, limbs,
the handiwork of retired warlords and
drug smuggling bankers.
He sipped
milk slowly through
a straw to ease his ulcer,
the American way.
Metal fragments rip through
the lawn
of the traffic meridian,
the American way,
erosion of public support
making politicians break out in cold sweat
and four-star generals' blood boil.
Meanwhile, children give each other
their favorite toys.
In the sand zone between
high and low tides,
among the wave-eroded rocks,
tidal pools, each a universe in itself,

and further up the dunes,
some parts of which the wind and snow
have twisted into strange shapes,
the ground bristles with
slender brushwood, a habitat
for thousands of rarely-seen creatures.
Next year this will be
a luxury hotel and golf course,
privatized by the corporations,
the American way.
Along meandering rivers
cottonwood and willows still thrive,
caterpillar tents in wild cherry trees
in the spring,
sunny openings in the canopy,
turbulence above the treeline,
a pressure-cooker environment below.
While along garden walks
and succulent terraces
the rules of engagement
strike a row of homes.
All the great works of western civilization,
written on the wings of
small nondescript brownish moths,
remain powerless to reveal
the full depths of deceit
and the full light of truth,
the American way.

ON A DAY LIKE TONIGHT IN AMERICA

On a night like today in America,
the almost-full moon
casting shadows behind us,
beating the brilliant drums
dancing through the chaparral hills.
On a day of zero visibility,
sandstorms engulfing the TV gossip columns,
overweight accountants rolling
shopping carts over concrete rubble,
comatose custodians
raising the rags upside down,
defiant frogs flipping birds,
calico cats pissing sideways
on no trespassing signs,
scarred teenagers roaming the alleys
handcuffing landlords and realtors,
scarlet tanagers hurling themselves
against barbed wire police
station windows and doors.
Neighbors pour dog
shit into stuffed ballot boxes,
while over 157,000 children
still languish in refugee camps
behind old city hall.
Meanwhile they unearth the mass
graves in the abandoned orchard, decomposing
bodies intertwined

into cherry tree roots,
some still wearing socks.
In the scorched plaza the revenging angels
bleach the robes of the kneeling judges
with their own lies and impunity.
They order the F.B.I and mafia
to remove each other's
hobnailed alligator loafers.
They tie up the blindfolded bankers
with their own elastic silk garters,
line up the lawyers in size place
according to the magnitude
of their crimes.
With the harvest moon
casting brilliant shadows behind us,
we danced through the chaparral hills
beating the drums of justice,
on a day like tonight,
in America
on a night like today.

AMERICAN ROULETTE

We owe nothing to the banks
we owe nothing to the corporations
the only national debt we owe
is to the unborn generations.

Or spin the cylinder,
point the barrel at your head,
no regret,
don't fret,
no sweat,
everybody wins
at American roulette.

Thirty or forty some-odd trillion
or whatever it is today,
plus millions more in
interest every minute.
What they call "the national debt."
It's really just a game of chance.
Numbers on a screen.

We borrowed all that green
from the banks and corporations,
—or so the pundits tell us—
to finance our security,
the endless wars
we wage to secure a world

of unlimited benefits for
the banks and corporations.

Here we are, the richest
country in the history of the world,
but we can barely afford living.
Into the burning pits,
entire loving families,
dumped arbitrarily along with
the smoldering husks of
looted grocery stores and restaurants.
Walking about the old neighborhood
means courting death, but
emergency rooms deny
anyone without proper papers.
The only items seemingly left untouched
are the parking meters and ATMs.

Spin the cylinder,
point the barrel at your head,
no regret,
don't fret,
no sweat,
it's on the House and
when the House always wins,
everybody wins
at American roulette.

Bank mercenaries deployed on roofs,

snipers arbitrarily picking off anyone who
moves too fast or too slow.
Deputies hurling gasoline bombs
into all the barber shops.
Shortages of water, thought, medicine,
integrity, compassion.
Municipal workers pretend to
sweep up the broken plate glass
and body parts, while
in the sidewalk cafes,
constables and elected officials
still exchange makeup tips.
Suddenly ragged young girls
emerge from the alleys
throwing rocks, bottles
and honesty.

We owe nothing to the banks
we owe nothing to the corporations
the only national debt we owe
is to the unborn generations.

AMERICAN MAKE-BELIEVE

Lips meet passionate lips
in the nuanced shadows
gorgeous bodies intertwined
ecstatic dance joyful tears
soulful communion
forever whispering
infinite vows devoted depths.
Flip on the lights
giant screen torn and ragged
musty stale popcorn
rancid imitation butter
rows of empty seats
spilled soda
garbage all over the floor
smells like piss.
American make-believe.
Grammas dry their tears
with candidates' promises
scribbled on shredded ballots,
nominees all promising
home love integrity prosperity
bouquets of imaginary hot jobs
blueberry syrup avatars
on every cyber maple pancake,
belief in change and bereavement,
a young couple on a first date
pulled over by officers

in front of the high-tech playground
for reasons unclear in the report,
find their fashion-statement purse
and plastic leather wallet confiscated,
photoshopped evidence
planted in every pocket
their late-model legoland SUV hijacked
every secret digital code of decency
systematically violated
orifices stuffed with sweaty junk
and auctioned to the highest bidder
while the duly-elected mayor
restoring public order
describes the peaceful demonstration
as an organized conspiracy
of arson and looting,
but it's only American make-believe.
In the wake of three weeks of
indiscriminate bombardment
and revenge killings,
stealing fingers for souvenirs,
leaving the remnants of
the once-stately city center
in control of stylish pimps
drugged lieutenants
spitting strawbosses
TV detectives
psychotic anchormen
corrupted weathergirls flush with

sunny gusts in the 10-day forecast,
while vomit gas permeates
all the side streets
removing children's souls,
thousands wounded, unknown dead

the masked soldiers
open fire on the hospital,
the crowd scatters, hundreds trampled,
she watches her friend's leg blown off,
while not far away
they stand for hours in the freezing rain
to exercise their sacred right to vote,
but just kidding,
it's only American make-believe.

UN-AMERICAN

As un-American as these songs in the night
as the meadow jumping mouse and
                    the red-legged frog
as the dark cloud hanging over the spot
where the pipeline burst into flames
as plant closings and layoffs
as un-American as unnamed
                    administration sources
as the candidate pulling a fast one
as a hissing noise in the Lincoln bedroom
as unmarked graves
bureaucratic delays
toxic substances in natural foods
as barbed wire around playgrounds
as children panhandling in front
                    of the drug store
as un-American as everywhere feelings of
helplessness, confusion, despair
as un-American as entering the mall
                    in a camouflage vest
as afterward turning the gun on himself
as the view from Andromeda galaxy
as newlywed dandelions
as kissing under the willow tree
as damselflies swooping through bulrushes
as strings of beads of silver, turquoise,
                    coral, shell

as the future of labor in the visions
of teenage revolutionaries
as un-American as family farm seeds
secretly handed down from generation to
generation like heirlooms
as un-American as restoring balance
as un-American as
every spot on earth is sacred.

AMERICAN TRANSITIONS

transition of deputies dumping
           furniture on sidewalk
transition of graft in brief case to politician
transition of knife through skin
transition of finger into eye
transition from knee to groin
transition from electrode to brain
transition of cop club through skull
transition from school to bomb crater
transition from loved one to body parts
transition from submit to fight back
transition from dream to wake
transition of fist through wall
transition of rock
       through cop car windshield
transition of neighbors carrying
       furniture back into home
transition of politician to rogues gallery
transition from garbage to compost
transition from rubble to new school
transition of homeless to neighborhood
transition from resist to transform
transition from wave to shore
transition from laugh to cry
transition of winter to spring
transition from fall to fly
transition from flower to seed

transition of summer to fall
transition from wake to dream
transition from floor to wall
transition of rain to snow
transition of snow to sleet
transition from branch to sprout
transition from cook to eat
transition from sprout to leaf
transition from cloud to air
transition from brown seed
                              to green shoot
transition from here to there
transition from poverty to collectivity
transition from asteroid to comet
transition from isolate to socialize
transition from corporate to commons
transition from kiss to talk
transition from talk back to kiss
transition from lips to tongue
transition from tongue back to lips
transition from hips to genitals
transition from genitals back to hips
transition from genital to genital
transition from hips to hips

AMERICAN TURNOVERS

Now all things American overturn.
Seamstresses unravel socks
carpenters nail their hammers
omelets flip themselves over
houses balance on their roof ridges
tree roots stretch into the air
cumulous clouds billow into back yards
senior execs pull each others' comb-overs
FBI agents bug each others' phones
peace officers club each other
                            over the head
incumbent officeholders change
                               their names
the president's cabinet put on
                        false mustaches
the Chamber of Commerce sniff
                        brown paper bags
Secretary of the Interior hides in the closet
head of ICE slips through the airport in drag
CEOs arrive in the Cayman Islands
the two-party system is under
arrest for impersonating democracy,
and all the payoffs of all
the corporate lobbyists
can't buy a jelly sandwich.

Turnovers: Semicircular pastries made

by turning one half of a circular crust over
the other, enclosing the filling,
usually fruit.

Spurning career politicians
churning seas undertow ownership patents
burning corporate papers
turning over unjust laws.
overturning privatized commons
America overturns:
Overturn a brand new leaf,
leaf through a dog-eared book,
book the d.a. for felony graft,
graft a plum branch onto a peach root,
root out the causes of social strife,
strive toward revelatory visions,
envision the end of bureaucratic dictators,
dictate a hundred songs about love,
love the work you live,
live for wholeness and light,
light the fires of forgiveness,
forgive the failings of your parents,
parent your children to interconnections,
interconnect compassion to your world,
world consciousness overturns
American turnovers.

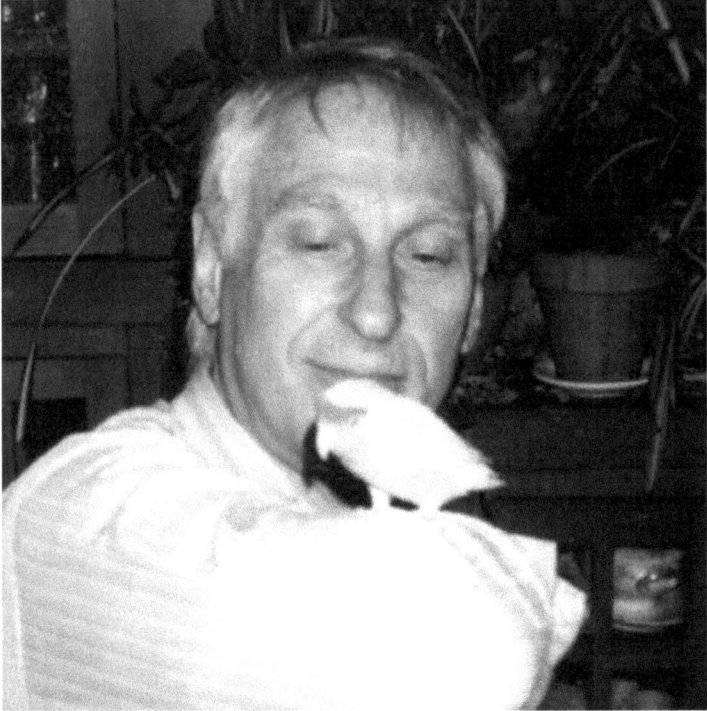

ABOUT THE AUTHOR

I am author of twelve poetry collections, two novels, a memoir, and several histories. My translations of Inca, Maya, and Aztec poets are collected in *Ancient American Poets*. I was one of the founders of Indigenous Peoples Day in 1992, and have worked on the Berkeley powwow since then. Born in New York City in 1940, my family was a mixture of Romanian-Austrian Jew, Irish Catholic, English-Scottish Protestant, French and German. During the winters I grew up in Manhattan, and during the summers in New Jersey farm country without electricity or running water. My father was a post office worker, and my mother had been a dancer in Broadway musicals. I have a degree in Comparative Literature from New York City College, with a semester at the Sorbonne in Paris, France. I reside in Berkeley and have one daughter. I was a professional woodworker and cabinetmaker for over forty years at Heartwood Cooperative Woodshop. I served as chair of West Berkeley Artisans and Industrial Companies, and as a Berkeley planning commissioner. I was vice-president of PEN Oakland. My play *The Trial of Christopher Columbus* was produced by the Writers Theater in 2009. My transliterations from Pachacuti's Quechua formed the libretto for Tania León's *Ancient* (2009). I represented the USA at the World Poetry Festival in 2010 in Caracas, Venezuela. I have been a member of the Revolutionary Poets Brigade of San Francisco for many years, and an editor of their annual anthologies.

website:
https://johncurl.net/

ALSO BY JOHN CURL

Poetry:
Memory of a Kiss (Homeward Press, 2025)
Rainbow Weather (Vagabond Books, 2022)
Yoga Sutras of Fidel Castro (Homeward Press, 2014)
Revolutionary Alchemy (Homeward Press, 2012)
Scorched Birth (Beatitude Press, 2004)
Columbus in the Bay of Pigs (Inkworks /Homeward, 1991)
Decade (Mother's Hen, 1987)
Tidal News (Homeward Press, 1982)
Cosmic Athletics (Poetry For The People, 1980)
Ride the Wind (Poetry For The People, 1979)
Spring Ritual (Cloud House, 1978)
Insurrection/Resurrection (Working People's Artists, 1975)
Commu 1 (Gnosis Press, 1971)
Change/Tears (Drop City, 1967)

Poetry Translation:
Ancient American Poets (Bilingual Press, 2005).

Memoir:
Memories of Drop City (Homeward Press, 2008).

History:
Indigenous Peoples Day (IPD Books, 2017)
For All The People (PM Press, 2009, 2012)
History of Collectivity in the San Francisco Bay Area
                              (Homeward Press, 1982)
History of Work Cooperation in America
                              (Homeward Press, 1980).

Fiction:
The Outlaws of Maroon (Homeward Press, 2019)
The Coop Conspiracy (Homeward Press, 2014)

HOMEWARD
PRESS

www.ingramcontent.com/pod-product-compliance
Lightning Source LLC
Chambersburg PA
CBHW051707090426
42736CB00013B/2575